Fortnite:

Legendary Guide to becoming a Pro in Fortnite Battle Royale

Table of Contents

The follow book is reproduced below with the goal of providing information that is as accurate and reliable as possible. Regardless, purchasing this book can be seen as consent to the fact that both the publisher and the author of this book are in no way experts on the topics discussed within and that any recommendations or suggestions that are made herein are for entertainment purposes only. Professionals should be consulted as needed prior to undertaking any of the action endorsed herein.

This declaration is deemed fair and valid by both the American Bar Association and the Committee of Publishers Association and is legally binding throughout the United States.

Furthermore, the transmission, duplication or reproduction of any of the following work including specific information will be considered an illegal act irrespective of if it is done electronically or in print. This extends to creating a secondary or tertiary copy of the

Introduction

Congratulations on downloading *Fortnite: Legendary Guide to becoming a Pro in Fortnite Battle Royale* and thank you for doing so. *Fortnite*: *Battle Royale* is the free-to-play multiplayer component of a less than successful Minecraft clone that has taken the world by storm in the months since its release with its take on the one versus 100 genre, with a dash of building thrown in. With everyone from celebrities to your little brother thoroughly addicted to the game, it can be easy to want to be good at it, in fact, it can be easy to want to be the very best.

Unfortunately for those who are arriving a little late to the party, there are plenty of people out there who are already very, very good at *Fortnite*. Luckily, the following chapters will discuss everything you need to know in order to take your game to the next level in no time flat, starting with the way in which many people come to the game which is as a *PUBG* player who is tired of hearing about the next big thing. Next, you will learn all about the best starting locations for a new game, as well as how to reach those spots as fast as possible through judicious glider use.

From there you will learn all about how to earn as much free stuff in the game as possible by maximizing your V-buck rewards. You will then learn a wide variety of advanced tips and tricks to take your game to the next level, before learning several tips focused specifically on building better as well. Finally, you will learn an extremely effective strategy when it comes to earning your first solo win.

There are plenty of books on this subject on the market, thanks again for choosing this one! Every effort was made to ensure it is full of as much useful information as possible, please enjoy!

Chapter 1: Transitioning from PUBG to Fortnite

If you are a *PlayerUnknown's Battlegrounds* player who is more than a little curious about Epic's take on the Battle Royale formula, you aren't alone. In fact, many people are already calling *Fortnite* the heir apparent to *PUBG's* throne. Regardless of whether or not this is true, *Fortnite* has managed to change up the traditional formula in some interesting ways, while also speeding things up in a way that doesn't necessarily feel like simplification for simplification's sake.

If you enjoy *PUBG* but haven't yet given *Fortnite* a try, then you can rest assured that, despite what purists, believe, it isn't just a blatant clone, as the building aspect of the game goes a surprising distance towards separating the two. Specifically, it ensures that you always have additional options to turn a bad situation around, regardless of what tools may be on hand. The map is also smaller overall, and that, plus the different visual style all combine in a way that makes the game feel different, if not exactly fresh. If you are considering jumping in (and why wouldn't you, it's free) keep the following tips in mind to help get over the learning curve that comes along with switching from one game to the other.

Get your expectations in check

First things first, when switching games, you are going to notice a wide variety of similarities, which will make the differences all that much more frustrating. While this is certainly a natural response, if you truly want to improve your experience then you need to be willing to understand and adapt to the differences, rather than disregarding strategies that don't appear obvious to you as someone who has played a lot of *PUBG*. Finally, if you do want to make the change successfully, be prepared to play for a few hours before things start to click.

Get to know building

The first thing you need to understand about *Fortnite* as a *PUBG* player is that building is key. With the proper skill, you will literally be able to build circles around your opponents, making the moment where you move in for the kill almost an afterthought. As you move throughout the world you will find materials, just as you would weapons, equipment and the like, and you can also collect them by hitting buildings with your pickax. As you are going to want to stock up on crafting materials early on, the first thing you will want to keep in mind is the early game should be as much about getting crafting materials as it is a decent gun.

Another important thing you are going to want to keep in mind when it comes to building is that your character doesn't actually build the objects you place, which means you can move on as soon as the building process has begun. As such, if someone is shooting at you, throwing down the first piece of wall will be enough to provide you limited cover before it is even fully formed. It also means that you can build stairs as you are running up them, virtually guaranteeing if you see an overhead space, you can reach it with staircases as long as you have the required building materials.

Practically, what all this added mobility means is that, unlike in *PUBG,* in *Fortnite* you are never at the mercy of the map, which means you need to spend more time thinking about the potential of the space you are in rather than considering how to make do with what is available. Of course, this does involve becoming competent with the building menu to the point where you can choose the structure you are looking to build and the building material, without slowing down. As you can bet that a majority of the players around you are going to be able to build without slowing down, learning this nuance of the game should be your top priority.

Finally, it is important to keep in mind that building makes noise that other players can hear. What's more, anything you build is going to clearly standout out against the map as well. While building can certainly provide you with the extra edge you need to come out on top in a battle, it will also make you a target and learning how best to balance this risk and reward will only come with time.

Understanding inventory

Another big difference between the two games is the way that *Fortnite* handles inventory. Specifically, each character has a total of five inventory slots, no less and no more. This will naturally mean that you have to do a lot more inventory management than you would in *PUBG*, but luckily there are some other changes that make this process less cumbersome than it might appear at first blush.

Likewise, while it can take some players dozens of hours to get comfortable with all the ins and outs of *PUBG*'s guns, *Fortnite* has perhaps simplified here more than anywhere else. The types of guns are far more general, with basic classes of guns such as shotgun or sniper rifle dropping with varying degrees of color coded rarity, using the Blizzard model of gray, green, blue, purple and orange with gray items being common and orange items dropping infrequently. As an added bonus, each successful kill will reward you with a veritable loot piñata as your fallen opponent's items explode off their downed body.

As such, you only need to really focus on weapons types that you like the most, with something short, medium and long range always a good choice as you would imagine. Once you are comfortable with your standard loadout, all you then need to do is focus on getting guns that are a better color than what you currently have available and you are good to go. Of special importance to note is the relative increase in power level that all short-ranged guns have in *Fortnite* as compared to *PUBG*. Regardless of your thoughts on shotguns in *PUBG*, pick one up in *Fortnite*, you will be glad you did.

Finally, you will want to round out your inventory with shields or healing items and go to town.

Keep in mind the differences in pacing

While you could easily spend upwards of 30 minutes in *PUBG* without seeing another person, living or dead, a game of *Fortnite* is a much more rambunctious affair. Things tend to play out much more quickly, and once you get used to your run speed you should never have a hard time staying within the circle. Keep in mind there are no vehicles in *Fortnite* either, so you don't need to keep and ear out in the distance for them as well. Focus on what's in front of you, and focus on the short game first, and you will find your time spent with *Fortnite* is much improved.

Chapter 2: Starting out Strong

Best Landing Spots

The way you start off a game of *Fortnite* is going to frequently dictate your experience throughout the match which means that choosing the ideal starting spot will go a long way towards increasing your odds of finding a place in the final circle, what you do there, of course, is up to you. Landing in a bad spot could lead you to a risky position where you struggle to find loot before everyone else does and still end up with nothing compared to the player that ends your run with all the legendary loot you couldn't seem to snag.

While the map might look small, there is a surprisingly large amount of ground to cover which means that choosing the best landing spots that have the highest loot drops is critical to success in both the short and the long term.

East of Haunted Hills and Junk Junction

In the top left of the map you should see both Haunted Hills and Junk Junction near the corner. Just to the right of this location is a cluster of ruined houses that are known to contain higher than average rarity drops. If you can make it to this location first, you can find multiple golden chests ripe for the picking. From there, you can move over to Haunted Hills or Junk Junction proper, though Pleasant Park is known to have a better drop rate overall if you have the time to make it there. Depending on how much time has passed, these three locations are likely going to be full of players as well, but with your golden chest loot, you should be up for the challenge.

Near Flush Factory and Shifty Shafts

If you have landed near either Flush Factory or Shifty Shafts, then you have likely seen the huge wooden chair sitting near a few houses and a diner that's seen better days. While the quality of the drops you see here is going to vary, it will typically be enough to provide you with a full loadout, without having to waste time scouring multiple locations. The abandoned house also contains a chest along with plenty of trees nearby to allow you to stock up on crafting materials. Once you've cleaned up, you will then be able to move on to either Shifty Shafts or Flush Factory, as is your preference, and take out the players who dropped there first and are thus embroiled in a fight to control the area's loot.

Other side of Flush Factory

Directly to the right of Flush Factory you will find an area that frequently contains plenty of loot. As there are plenty of other opportunities around, however, this literal treasure trove often goes unnoticed. This is a shame, as running around in this area will practically guarantee you never stop hearing the sound cue that tells you a chest is nearby. As an added bonus, this area is also lousy with wooden pallets which give you a surprising amount of wood per pallet, to ensure you are ready to go in no time flat.

By Anarchy Acres

If you drop near Anarchy Acres and then float directly to your left, you should find yourself near a motel that is known for its quality loot. If you plan on landing here, however, be ready for a fight as it is already gaining a reputation for being one of the map's more popular landing spots. To ensure you come out on top, you are going to want to land on the abandoned houses nearby before working your way towards the motel. Use the gaps in the walls to get the drop on your opponents and stick to the rooftops if possible. Once you reach the motel, keep an ear out for chests and don't forget the trucks outside as they sometimes spawn chests as well.

Land faster

Once you have a good idea of where you want to go, the next thing you are going to want to do is to ensure that you get there as quickly as possible. While it is poorly explained, the truth of the matter is that you can land up to 10 seconds faster than other players, if you follow the tips outlined below. It doesn't take much tactical genius to understand how this can lead to a significant advantage in the opening seconds of the match that can often set the stage for much of what is to come.

To land faster than the competition, all you need to do is start by choosing a landing location but avoid jumping for it when you are directly above it. Instead, you are going to want to know where you are headed early on so that you can divebomb into an area that is close by, before gliding to your desired location. The crucial part of this maneuver at this stage is to avoid any elevated terrain to ensure a quick landing. Flying too close to one of these hazards will automatically trigger your parachute and ruin your fun. Instead, you will want to aim for the lowest point on the horizon for the best results.

Your end goal will then be deploying your parachute when you are initially close to the ground before gliding towards your ultimate destination, as opposed to gently floating down like a chump. While you may misjudge at first, it should only take a few drops for you to get the hang of the timing to land at all the most popular spots on the map.

Common myths debunked

While we are at it, there are numerous different myths surrounding what causes an increased drop rate, so keep in mind that when you hear anyone swearing that any of the following works, they are sadly mistaken.

- Dropping straight on top of a target and then holding forward and down isn't a faster way to drop and actually results in you dropping slower.
- Gliders are not upgradeable.
- Umbrellas are purely cosmetic
- All gliders have the same functionality, all changes are purely cosmetic.

Chapter 3: Maximize Your V-Buck Rewards

While *Fortnite* is experiencing a massive popularity boom, it still needs to cover the cost of ongoing development and continued maintenance, especially as Epic scrapped all their other games to focus on it exclusively. Luckily, *Fortnite* avoids the potentially destructive snafu that other games have suffered from in recent memory and avoids any type of pay to win scenario, focusing purely on cosmetic rewards instead.

This currency is known as V-Bucks and it can be used for a variety of cosmetic items including things like new harvesting tools, gliders, and character skins to give your play the stylish boost you need to take you to the next level. While you can certainly plop down a fat wad of cash for a large stack of V-Bucks, you can also earn them in-game without paying for them, assuming you paid for the full version of the game at least. You did know that *Fortnite* had a single-player component, didn't you? Assuming you have the single-player version, you can score free V-bucks in a number of ways.

Daily log-in bonus

While it won't net you much each day, you can receive free V-bucks each day by simply logging into the single-player mode of the game. This bonus is available each and every day, so it adds up more quickly than you might expect, especially if you are taking the other tips on this list to heart as well. Even better, if you continue to log in regularly, you get bonus V-Bucks on a variety of different days. These bonuses keep going, even if you miss a day and include bonuses of 300, 500, 800, and even 1,000 V-Bucks.

Daily quests

In addition to your daily login bonus, you can also actually commit to playing the single-player version of *Fortnite* and you will get a new quest every day. What follows is a list of the daily quests as well as the reward for completing each of them.

- Daily Destroy (Arcade Machines) - Destroy 6 Arcade Machines in successful missions (often found in City zones) - 50 V-Bucks
- Daily Destroy (Fire Trucks) - Destroy 3 Fire Trucks in successful missions (often found in City zones) - 50 V-Bucks

- Daily Destroy (Garden Gnomes) - Destroy 3 Garden Gnomes in successful missions (often found hidden in every zone) - 50 V-Bucks
- Daily Destroy (Park Seesaws) - Destroy 8 Park Seesaws in successful missions (often found in Suburban zones) - 50 V-Bucks
- Daily Destroy (Propane Tanks) - Destroy 10 Propane Tanks in successful missions (often found in Industrial zones) - 50 V-Bucks
- Daily Destroy (Server Racks) - Destroy 4 Server Racks in successful missions (often found in Bunkers and Shelters) - 50 V-Bucks
- Daily Destroy (Teddy Bears) - Destroy 8 Teddy Bears in successful missions (often found in Suburban zones) - 50 V-Bucks
- Daily Destroy (TVs) - Destroy 20 TVs in successful missions (often found in Suburban zones) - 50 V-Bucks
- Daily Scouting Cities - Discover 10 City Locations; Police Stations, Fire Stations, Hospitals, Parking Lots and Decks - 50 V-Bucks
- Daily Scouting Industrial Construction - Discover 5 Industrial Construction Sites - 50 V-Bucks

- Daily Scouting Rural - Discover 6 Rural Locations; Bunkers, Shacks and Ruined Houses (found in Forests and Grasslands) - 50 V-Bucks
- Daily Scouting Shelters - Discover 8 Outdoor Survivor Shelters (found in all zones) - 50 V-Bucks
- Husk Extermination (Any Hero) - Kill 500 Husks (Any Hero) in successful missions - 50 V-Bucks
- Husk Exterminator (Constructor) - Kill 500 Husks in successful missions as a Constructor - 50 V-Bucks
- Husk Exterminator (Ninja) - Kill 500 Husks in successful missions as a Ninja - 50 V-Bucks
- Husk Exterminator (Outlander) - Kill 500 Husks in successful missions as a Outlander - 50 V-Bucks
- Husk Exterminator (Soldier) - Kill 500 Husks in successful missions as a Soldier - 50 V-Bucks
- Mission Specialist (Constructor) - Complete 3 missions as a Constructor 50 V-Bucks
- Mission Specialist (Ninja) - Complete 3 missions as a Ninja - 50 V-Bucks
- Mission Specialist (Outlander) - Complete 3 missions as an Outlander - 50 V-Bucks

- Mission Specialist (Soldier) - Complete 3 missions as a Soldier - 50 V-Bucks
- Mission Specialist (Stonewood) - Complete 3 missions in Stonewood - 50 V-Bucks
- Mission Specialist (Plankerton) - Complete 3 missions in Plankerton - 60 V-Bucks
- Mission Specialist (Canny Valley) - Complete 3 missions in Canny Valley - 75 V-Bucks
- Mission Specialist (Twine Peaks) - Complete 3 missions in Twine Peaks - 100 V-Bucks
- A Little Van That Could! - Complete 3 Ride the Lightning missions - 50 V-Bucks
- Data Retrieval - Complete 3 Retrieve the Data missions - 50 V-Bucks
- Storm Chaser - Complete 3 Fight the Storm missions - 50 V-Bucks
- All Together Now - Complete 3 Play with Others missions - 50 V-Bucks
- Party Of 25 - Save 25 Survivors in successful missions - 50 V-Bucks

Chapter 4: Advanced Tips and Tricks

When it comes to doing everything they can in order to earn that star prize, it can be easy for many players to get so focused on the complexities of high-level play that don't focus enough on ensuring that their fundamentals are perfected to their absolute apex. What follows is a mix of tips and tricks that are is easy to miss including habits you need to form and mechanics that you want to start practicing with sooner rather than later if you truly want to start racking up those wins.

Change the key bindings

One of the biggest giveaways that the Battle Royale mode of *Fortnite* was an afterthought is the fact that the default key bindings leave building on the PC feeling incredibly frustrating. Luckily, Epic realized the mess they had made and don't have any qualms about allowing players to rebind their keys to their heart's content. This can be done from the options menu, using the Input Tab and then selecting Building Options.

While you can bind the keys in any way you like, for simplicity's sake you may find it useful to keep in mind that traditional walls come pre-bound to Q, so you are going to want to pick other keys that are close to WASD to ensure you can move while getting your building done as well. F and V are two common choices, as they ensure your fingers don't have far to move during the frantic end-game. While this new arrangement may be strange at first, especially if you have already spent some time learning the default keys, with practice, you will see your build speed soar thanks to the new keys.

Don't ignore launch pads

While it might be easy to downplay the effectiveness of the launch pad with the ease of building naturally standing in for most mobility needs, the fact of the matter is a well-placed jump pad can easily allow you to pull victory from the jaws of defeat. All you need to do to activate it is to set it down on a flat surface and hop on to be shot into the air and allowed to deploy your parachute. Once airborne, you can even tuck your parachute back in and redeploy it to help you avoid taking damage from an enemy who saw you take to the skies. You can also use a launch pad to escape from a blue zone that is fast approaching, retreat from a fight or even take the fight to a surprised enemy.

Pickaxe equals faster looting

This tip is as simple as it is effective. Whenever you find yourself staring down a large load of loot, do yourself a favor and equip your pickaxe before you start interacting with any of it. Doing so will ensure that you pick up each and every last morsel of ammo without swapping out any of your weapons by mistake.

Learn how the guns work

In many more realistic shooters, such as *PUBG* for example, whenever you fire a gun, the physics of a real bullet is mimicked, and the bullet drops the further it travels. This leads to the required understanding of complicated mathematical formulas to ensure you aim at the right height to ensure that a bullet drops enough to hit a player's head when you need it to.

Fortnite decided that this was all too much, and chose instead to make all of the guns, save for sniper rifles, operate via what is known as a hit-scan model instead. What this means, is that if you are pointing a gun at someone when you pull the trigger, your bullet will hit them instantly. As hit-scan guns are used far less these days than they once were, most players don't even consider this a possibility, which causes them to spend far more time lining up their shots than they actually need to. Take advantage of this and mow them down where they stand.

Pay more attention to crates

A surprising number of ammo crates are left untouched at the end of each round. Remember, stocking up on ammo, especially when it is so readily available, can be the difference between success and failure. Remember, if you have ammo to burn you can break through structures much more quickly than your enemies are expecting, catching them unawares in the process.

Unlike ammo crates, supply crates are always a high priority target for any player that sees them, and with good reason as they often contain loot that can completely turn the tide of battle. Luckily, you can get an edge on the competition by tracking the crate's location from the moment you see it. To do so, all you need to do is to shoot it as it is falling from the sky and then track it by following its health bar which should now be visible.

Start making counter plays

When you come face to face with an opponent, you will find far greater success if you think of each action you take as a counter to what your opponent is doing in an effort to counter your opponent's strategies, as opposed to simply flying by the seat of your pants in an effort to remain alive. For example, if they build a ramp above you, start building a roof with an adjacent doorway so you can reset the fight on your terms. If they start building a ramp up to your location, don't let them come to you, build upwards and over where they are coming from to leave them back at square one.

Getting used to a counter-play strategy is a two-part process. First, you will need to start thinking about the counter-plays that you could be using in a given situation and second, you will need to start considering those strategies quickly enough that you can act on them in a way that is able to impact the outcome of a given fight. Give it time, and be willing to practice, and soon you will find that you are able to think on your feet more effectively and end the game in a higher position as a result.

Always choose wood

Whenever you are building anything in a pinch, wood should always be the material you choose, bar none. While brick and metal are stronger, in theory, the truth of the matter is that a wooden wall can take two shotgun shell blasts at close range while metal and brick shatter after just one. This is a counter-intuitive fact that can save your life in high impact scenarios.

Try multiples of your favorite weapon

While the limited storage space provided to each character can make the best choice seem to be weapons that favor diversity, the opposite can often be true as well. Specifically, players have been seeing great success using either a pair of pump-action shotguns or bolt-action sniper rifles. Equipping two of either of these essentially allows you to eliminate any and all delay between reloading, allowing you to fire virtually twice in a row with practice by shooting one gun, hot swapping and shooting again. Your target will never know what hit them.

Chapter 5: Build Better

As previously noted, if there is one thing you are going to want to go out of your way to master when it comes to improving your *Fortnite* game, its building structures when you are in the direst need. In fact, if you watch the most successful players, time and again, then you will almost always find that they are able to place their structures in no-time flat.

While it can take some practice to really get up to speed, once you get the hang of putting together structures on the fly you will find that your games start lasting longer, guaranteed. In order to improve your building game as quickly as possible, keep the following tips in mind.

Watch the pros

While watching experts is rarely a way to make measurable improvements yourself, in this case, you can learn a surprising amount from watching those who are at the top of the game. While this won't allow you to directly increase your speed, per say, it will allow you to consider alternative types of structures you might not have considered beforehand which could be enough to put you over the edge. When watching these players, it is important to keep in mind that they rarely go for elaborate structures, instead preferring form over function, which is something you should do as well.

Useful structures for any scenario

While all of the following structures are sure to save your life at some point or another, it is important to keep in mind that you can only build them if you have the materials to do so. As such, it is important to get into an early habit of taking any spare moment you have to add to your resource pool. The first time you don't run out of materials at a key moment, you will be glad you did. This goes hand in hand with learning to keep an eye on your resources once you are in the middle of the fight to ensure you aren't left with any unfortunate surprises.

Walls

Walls are the most simple and easy to construct structures possible, yet despite that fact, many players still don't use them nearly enough. Simply put, you can always use more walls. Walls behind you will protect you when you are performing a tactical retreat while walls ahead of you can work as bullet sponges to give you the extra boost to finish off your opponent once and for all. As previously noted, you can't do better than the wooden wall, so the default option is almost always going to do you right.

Ramps

Another core building staple is the ramp as height advantage is something you are always going to want to take as much of as possible. What's more, you can duck behind the edge of the ramp for cover and peek over the edge to line up your shots for a simple and effective strategy that can be used to hold off multiple other players at once. It is easy to destroy, however, so any one ramp is never going to be more than a temporary safe haven.

One ramp advantage that is often overlooked by new players is the obvious benefit of building a ramp scenario when you've spotted an enemy moving towards you in the distance. You can get started quickly and easily by first throwing down a handful of walls to create a box before standing in the middle and creating a ramp that leads upward. To finish off your safe spot all you need to do is place a wall at the back of the ramp.

From there, you can increase your advantage even more by, adding additional height advantage as well as the option to fire from two different points, ensuring your opponent never knows what to expect next. To proceed, all you need to do is stand on the top of your initial ramp and then build another box before placing a pair of ramps that lead up to two different points. This structure is virtually limitless when it comes to expansion opportunities, so it will allow you to expand as the encounter demands.

Sniper Tower

A classic sniper tower is a great choice when it comes to gaining some true height when you are looking to attack your enemies from afar. What's more, this tower can be put together in seconds, with practice, so you can be ready to snipe at the drop of a hat. When building any type of extended tower, it is important to always ensure that you have a clear exit in case you are swarmed with players peppering your tower with shots from all sides.

You can get this building started by first encasing yourself completely within a small box. From there, you will then want to choose a side and jump up, placing a ramp as you do so. From there, you just need to move to the highest point of the ramp, building walls as you do so. Repeat as needed. This same base can be used to scale in a wide variety of ways, from reaching inaccessible areas to creating impossible to reach castles in the sky, the choices are endless.

The Funnel

The funnel is a useful variation of the above ramp that can be used to either create a structure that has both cover and height advantage or a wide platform that can be used to give an entire team the ability to survey a wide area. To get started, all you need to do is build a 2 x 2 box before standing in the center and placing pyramids in each of the corners. The end result should look like a funnel that is sucking inwards.

Alternately, you can start by building stairs that protrude outwards from each of the walls before placing the pyramids, so they align between the gaps, this will make the overall funnel effect even larger. You can then add walls by simply running around the structure and placing them outside. You can do this from within the safety of the funnel which should end up providing you a fair amount of cover.

Edit after the fact

Don't forget, after you have placed a basic structure, such as a wall, you can then go ahead and edit it so that it becomes something else entirely. As an example, you can turn a wall into an archway, or even a door, which can completely change the flow of a fight, while it is still taking place. With practice, this type of move can see you easily outplaying your opponents.

Chapter 6: Solo Successfully

While walking away from the island alive is enough for some people, whatever the stakes, for others it is the desire for a solo win that keeps them up at night. While there are plenty of different options when it comes to soloing successfully, the following strategy has proven extremely successful for a variety of players, regardless of skill level.

Drops

There a couple different ways that you can drop into the field depending on personal preference. First, you can wait on the bus until the last few seconds and jump when no one else is jumping. Depending on your timing, this can score you some very good loot with little resistance. The biggest problem with this strategy is that it will see you running. A lot. You are basically at the mercy of the circle at this point and will have to run almost the entire game to stay alive. This is a strategy for those who prefer a nomadic playstyle as you will only get a chance to really dig in if you get lucky and the circle ends up falling in your favor.

Alternately, you can jump early on, as soon as you get an idea of the path the bus is going to be taking. With practice, you will know the map well enough that you will be able to see the trajectory and know which locations it will be flying over so you can plan your jumps according. Generally speaking, if you want to ensure that you are not at the mercy of the circle you are going to want to wait no longer than 20 seconds to jump. Once you jump and get close to your chosen location, it is perfectly fine to land on the outskirts if you feel as though things are going to get too spicy to quickly, most locations have outbuildings that you can scavenge through with loot to give you a fighting chance in the early game.

Early game

Once you are on solid ground, your next major task is grabbing yourself some gear. If you landed in a remote area, this task is easy, head to the nearest building and pick it clean. If you landed in a named location or a cluster of houses or building that somebody else may have landed in, you will need to make a mad dash for a gun. Any gun will do, you just need something to defend yourself with as otherwise, fights are going to get very lopsided, very quickly.

Once you have cleared the area or confirmed that no one is around, you can then proceed to loot. If you are outside the circle, get close to it, but don't worry about getting in it until the storm is pretty close behind you. One of the biggest mistake that new players make is overreacting to the storm and not focusing on more pressing matters like the other 99 players looking to kill them.

If you landed inside the circle, congrats! Loot your immediate buildings and avoid engagements if possible. Once you are properly geared up, you will want to find a place to hide as everyone else will be heading your way. In this scenario, bushes are your friends, in the right bush, you are essentially invisible. Just keep in mind, a bush is a very bad place to instigate an attack because most of the time, you are very, very open and bushes make terrible cover once other players know where you are. If you are waiting in a bush, it's best to adopt a shoot second approach.

Mid game

When it comes to choosing what loot to keep and what to toss, a good rule of thumb is to keep three slots for weapons, one for medical, and one for grenades or a launcher of some kind. If you are somewhere that is highly populated or are expecting a fight sooner than later you are going to want to pick up a secondary med kit or grenade, but, generally speaking, when you end up in a firefight, you'll need the extra firepower to keep you alive. Once an engagement is over and it's safe to loot a body, there is a good chance the other player's corpse have what you need to heal up.

Whenever you can grab grenades, a grenade launcher, or if you can manage it, a rocket launcher. Early on they will not prove especially useful, but towards the end of the round, the ability to destroy structures becomes imperative. Finally, you have three weapon slots to work with. Typically, you are going to want to personalize your loadout based on what works best for you, but you will want to have a mix of range and close-range firing potential. Don't be afraid to triple up on either shotguns or rifles, depending on personal preference, but you should avoid triple sniper rifles unless you have an extremely powerful locational advantage.

End game

At this point, you are in the circle, maybe the circle has moved in, and you have no choice but to move from your hiding place to keep up with it. Check your surroundings and go ahead and move. When you are close, or back in the circle, check your map, look at the size of the circle, and the surroundings, try to guess where the majority of the remaining players are coming from which you can do by considering which popular areas are close to the path of the circle. If you came from a densely populated area, try to hang back until you believe everyone has passed first and then move, waiting until the circle is almost on you again if you must. The idea is to stay behind people so that you are sure to see any potential threats before they see you.

If you are coming in from the less densely populated side, try to make your way around the edge of the circle rather than barreling straight through it. This is only a good choice if you can ensure with relative certainty that you can do so without being spotted. It's tactically advantageous to get behind the enemy, but you can't do that if they've already spotted you.

Once you've made it into the final 20 or 25 people, you can start moving a little faster towards the circle, especially if the game reached this point rather quickly. It is important to still try and remain hidden as best you can, while regularly checking behind you to watch for stragglers. Nevertheless, you are going to want to move into these final circles much more quickly than you did the early ones.

The biggest reason for this is going to be as a means of disrupting builders. Builders are people who have been farming resources the entire game with the goal of building an impregnable fortress in the absolute middle of the circle. While this strategy can be difficult to pull off successfully, when it works it can be difficult to play around, especially if you have been playing with the type of nomad strategy that this chapter recommends.

This is also why it is recommended that you spend one of your inventory slots on either grenades or rockets. As long as you have this option, the best strategy is to simply wait these players out and then get in the circle when they are distracted. As the circle grows smaller they will either have to leave or you can force them out.

Sniper rifles are effective here, if you kept one, but rifles will do the job as well. Get in close if you have grenades, but if this isn't an option, keep in mind you can always shoot a wall and still do damage to it, especially if it isn't made of wood. If you happened to secure a rocket launcher, well then go to town. Otherwise be patient, choose your shots carefully. Remember that if you're hidden well, you still shouldn't shoot first.

Now if you've made it into the final five, you might start to panic, don't worry, it happens to lots of people during their first time. If this is the case, then you will definitely want to take a second and calm down, just take things slow and remember to breath, it's just a game after all and if you made it to this point once, you can do it again. While doing so, you will want to check any potential cover above you as anyone up there will have tactical advantage over you which means they should be your top priority.

Above all else, you will want to try and stay hidden. The other players will also be looking for each other not only you, so if at all possible, let them fight it out. If you go full bore, make sure you have good cover readily available, and that you know where fire could come from on all sides. The final moments are always situational, but if you play your cards right, choose your shots, and have a good head on your shoulders, you can secure that win pretty easily.

Conclusion

Thank you for making it through to the end of *Fortnite: Legendary Guide to becoming a Pro in Fortnite Battle Royale*, let's hope it was informative and able to provide you with all of the tools you need to achieve your goals, whatever it is that they may be. Just because you've finished this book doesn't mean there is nothing left to learn on the topic, expanding your horizons is the only way to find the mastery you seek.

The next step is to stop reading already and to get started improving your *Fortnite* game. With so much useful information in hand, it can be easy to automatically assume that this will translate into increased performance. However, everything you have learned so far will only ever be as good as how much effort you work at putting these tips and tricks into practice. Ultimately, high level *Fortnite* play is a skill, which means that like any other skill it is only going to improve with practice.

As such, rather than jumping in and expecting to improve overnight, it will be far more effective to set a goal for your improvement, before using the tips described within to reach it using plenty of hard work and determination. Remember, improving at *Fortnite* is a marathon, not a sprint, slow and steady wins the race.

Finally, if you found this book useful in any way, a review on Amazon is always appreciated!